LEGENDS OF WARFARE
AVIATION

Curtiss P-40 Warhawk

The Famous Flying Tigers Fighter

DAVID DOYLE

Schiffer Publishing Ltd

4880 Lower Valley Road • Atglen, PA 19310

Designed by Justin Watkinson
Type set in Impact/Minion Pro/Univers LT Std

All photos are from the collections of the US National Archives and Records Administration unless otherwise noted.

ISBN: 978-0-7643-5432-8
Printed in China

Published by Schiffer Publishing, Ltd.
4880 Lower Valley Road
Atglen, PA 19310
Phone: (610) 593-1777; Fax: (610) 593-2002
E-mail: Info@schifferbooks.com
www.schifferbooks.com

For our complete selection of fine books on this and related subjects, please visit our website at www.schifferbooks.com. You may also write for a free catalog.

Schiffer Publishing's titles are available at special discounts for bulk purchases for sales promotions or premiums. Special editions, including personalized covers, corporate imprints, and excerpts, can be created in large quantities for special needs. For more information, contact the publisher.

We are always looking for people to write books on new and related subjects. If you have an idea for a book, please contact us at proposals@schifferbooks.com.

Acknowledgments

As with all of my projects, this book would not have been possible without the generous help of many friends. Instrumental to the completion of this book were Tom Kailbourn, Dana Bell, Scott Taylor, Stan Piet, Rich Kolasa, the staff of the National Archives and Records Administration, and Brett Stolle at the National Museum of the United States Air Force. Most importantly, I am grateful for the help and support of my wonderful wife Denise.

COVER: Curtiss P-40M 43-27483 was transferred to the Royal Canadian Air Force and redesignated Kittyhawk Mk IV serial number 845. Many years later, it was restored and remains in flying condition. Renamed *The Jacky C*, it currently resides at the American Airpower Museum, Farmingdale, New York. *Rich Kolasa*

Contents

Introduction

Although most often associated with a shark's teeth paint scheme and the Flying Tigers, the P-40 was used by the United States and her allies in every theater of World War II, and was used in combat for the duration of the war.

However, the design had its origins a full decade prior to V-J Day. The design can trace its roots to the Curtiss-Wright Model 75 pursuit plane, which was created by chief designer Donovan Berlin as a participant in a United States Army Air Corps (USAAC) pursuit competition held in May 1935. First flying in April 1935, the Model 75 was powered by a radial Wright XR-1670-5 radial engine. Because of difficulties with competitive aircraft, the completion was postponed a full year, until April 1936. During the delay, Wright modified the Model 75 through the installation of a Wright XR-1820-39, which was rated at 950-horsepower; fifty horsepower more than the previous powerplant, but more importantly also more reliable.

Even with this improvement, the Curtiss design lost the competition to the Seversky entry, although neither design met Army or design expectations. A contract was issued for seventy-seven of the Seversky aircraft, which were designated P-35.

However, only two months later, owing to the world situation and concerns about Seversky's ability to deliver aircraft in quantity, the USAAC ordered three service test examples of the Curtiss aircraft. These aircraft, designated Y1P-36 by the military and Model 75E by Curtiss, differed from the earlier version in having yet a different engine, this time the 900-horsepower Pratt & Whitney R-1830-13 Twin Wasp, the same engine as used on the P-35.

Yet another pursuit aircraft competition was held in May 1937, with the Curtiss Y1P-36 winning this round, and the company received a contract for 210 examples, designated P-36A. Additional examples were sold to numerous foreign nations, with France being the biggest buyer with 100 units.

Seeking improved performance, and intrigued by the possibility of a more streamlined cowl through the use of a liquid-cooled engine, the army requested that an aircraft be built using an Allison V-12 engine rather than a radial. Curtiss modified the original Model 75 with an Allison V-1710-11. The new aircraft was given the Curtiss model number 75I, and was designated the XP-37 by the Army Air Corps.

In order to accommodate the Allison and its associated cooling system, yet maintain balance, the cockpit was moved well to the rear, almost to the trailing edge of the wing.

This cockpit position led to poor visibility for the pilot, especially during take off, landing, and ground operation. Beyond those troubles, the performance of the aircraft, which first flew in April 1937, did not reach expectations.

However, enough potential existed for the Army to commit to thirteen service trial aircraft, designated YP-37, with a December 11, 1937 order. This aircraft would differ from the XP-37 in having a lengthened fuselage, a V-1710-21 engine and a General Electric B-2 supercharger. While an improvement over the XP-37, supercharger problems continued to plague the design and by early 1942, the type had been relegated to being teaching aids in mechanics schools.

CHAPTER 1
XP-40

The prototype for the Curtiss P-40s was the Curtiss Model 75P, which received the US Army Air Corps designation XP-40. It was based on the airframe of Curtiss P-36A 38-010 but with an Allison V-1710-19 water-cooled engine, with a streamlined cowl replacing the P-36A's air-cooled radial engine. The XP-40 made its first flight on October 14, 1938. This photo shows the plane at a later date after it had undergone modifications to its radiators. *Stan Piet collection*

Still not satisfied with the performance of the Allison-powered Curtiss, one more attempt was made. The tenth P-36A airframe, serial number 38-10, was selected to be powered by an Allison V-1710-19. Curtiss assigned Model 75P to the modified design, but the Army Air Corps designated the airplane the XP-40.

The first flight of the XP-40 was made on October 14, 1938, at the Curtiss plant in Buffalo, with test pilot Edward Elliot at the controls. Two days later, the aircraft was flown to Wright Field, Ohio, for evaluation. As with the XP-37, the Army was disappointed in the initial flight tests—weight and drag limited the XP-40's top speed to 324 mph.

Curtiss attempted to address these problems by relocating the radiator, but achieved little improvement. In an effort to find the definitive solution, Air Corps Fighter Projects Officer Lt. Ben Kelsey decided to involve the National Advisory Committee for Aeronautics (NACA) and their Langley Field, Virginia wind tunnel. The XP-40 was at Langley from March 28 to April 11, 1939.

Drawing on the results of these tests, the radiator intake was moved from a position beneath the fuselage and to the rear of the wing to directly behind and beneath the prop spinner. The new installation also included the oil cooler air intake. The landing gear doors were redesigned to decrease drag, and an improved exhaust system with individual exhaust ports for each cylinder, rather than a single exhaust for each bank, was introduced. With these changes, in December 1939, the XP-40 reached 366 mph. While, as with most designs, additional testing, especially at the NACA wind tunnel, could have brought about further improvements, the deteriorating world wide situation forced the Air Corps' hand.

After initial flight tests, the XP-40's radiators were moved forward to below the engine, occasioning a redesigned chin scoop and fairing for them. The engine was changed from the Allison V-1710-19 to the V-1710-33. Yet another engine-exhaust design was tested; the one seen here had two exhaust ducts. The XP-40, previously unarmed, now had two .50-caliber machine guns; the barrels are protruding through the fairings to the rear of the propeller.

In its initial configuration, the XP-40's radiators for the water-cooled Allison V-1710-19 engine were in a fairing on the belly of the fuselage to the rear of the cockpit. Also, initially, the engine exhausts were expelled through a single duct on each side of the fuselage. *National Museum of the United States Air Force*

The XP-40 is seen from the right side in its later configuration, with the radiators under the engine and two exhaust ducts on each side of the engine. The vertical tail was decorated with red and white horizontal stripes and a blue, vertical stripe.

The radiator fairing in its initial location is partially visible in this view of the XP-40 during a test flight. Various configurations of exhausts and exhaust fairings were tried on the XP-40, and in this photo a different design of fairing is present than in the preceding photo.

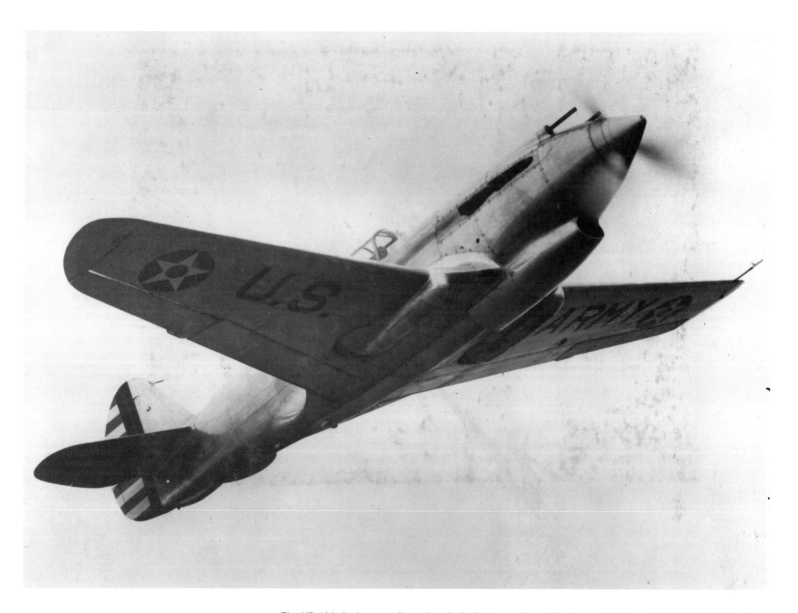

The XP-40 in its later configuration, including two exhaust ducts per side, is seen in flight. The bulged tail-wheel fairing and doors on the XP-40 were replaced on the production P-40-CU by flat doors. *National Museum of the United States Air Force*

CHAPTER 2
P-40(-CU)

The first production model of the Warhawk family of pursuit planes was the Curtiss P-40-CU, the "CU" being the manufacturer's code for Curtiss. Differences from the XP-40 included a larger, redesigned radiator fairing, which was also slightly farther forward; elimination of the bulged tail landing gear fairing and doors; and replacement of the carburetor air scoop with one of an entirely different design, located between the .50-caliber machine gun fairings. This model also had a .30-caliber machine gun in each wing. *National Museum of the United States Air Force*

Typical Air Corps procurement practice of the era was that experimental aircraft, usually one or two, that were designated with an X prefix, were followed by a small quantity, typically three to twelve service test aircraft, which carried a Y prefix, as was the case with the previously discussed YP-37.

With the precarious global situation, the Army Air Corps aimed to expand its force. On April 26, 1939, they ordered a number of service test examples of the Lockheed P-38 and Bell P-39—as well as 524 production examples of the P-40. Given the lower cost of the Curtiss product and the proven performance of the basic airframe in the form of the XP-36, the Air Corps felt justified in placing its largest (for that time) order for a pursuit aircraft. The contract was number AC-12414, and the Curtiss model number H81.

Various details differed between the XP-40 and the production aircraft, the latter being powered by a 1,040 horsepower V-1710-33 engine and armed with a pair of wing-mounted .30 caliber machine guns and a pair of cowl-mounted .50-caliber machine guns synchronized to fire through the propeller arc.

Rollout for the first production P-40, serial number 39-156, was March 18, 1940, in Buffalo, with the first flight occurring on April 4, 1940. Production aircraft began reaching service units in June, with the 33rd, 35th, and 36th Pursuit Squadrons of the 8th Pursuit Group at Langley Field being the first units equipped. The aircraft were almost immediately plagued with frequent ground-looping incidents. This tendency was traced to the combination of an Air Corps-mandated use of wing fillets smaller than those of the XP-40 and the Curtiss introduction of a cockpit air intake on the leading edge of each wing. For the rest of 1940, various fixes were developed and tried to resolve this issue, with varying results.

By September 1940, the Air Corps had taken delivery of 200 of the 524 aircraft ordered, at which time delivery of the balance was deferred to enable Curtiss to expedite French order F-273 for 140 H81A-1, an export version of the aircraft ordered on May 10, 1939. The H81A-1 was to be armed with two 7.5 mm FN-Browning machine guns, rather than one .30-caliber, in each wing, French-style seats that would accommodate the French parachutes, metric instruments, French radios, and a French-style throttle, which accelerated to the rear and closed to the front, opposite of US practice. France would fall before these aircraft were actually delivered, with the British purchasing them instead. With changes to bring the aircraft to British standards, such as replacing the wing machine guns with .303 Brownings, the aircraft were designated Tomahawk Is.

The US P-40s were further distinguished as P-40-CU in 1941 after the Air Corps mandated that a suffix identifying production facilities be added to model designations, with –CU being the identifier for the Curtiss Buffalo facility.

Curtiss delivered the first several P-40-CUs in highly polished, natural aluminum finish. "US ARMY" was marked on the bottoms of the wings. The round-shaped inlet of the carburetor air scoop is visible above and to the rear of the propeller spinner. Note how the radiator air scoop had two dividers inside it.

After the first several bare-aluminum P-40-CUs, Curtiss began delivering these planes painted in what was termed shadow camouflage, with Dark Olive Drab on the upper and side surfaces and Neutral Gray on the lower surfaces. At the rear of the radiator fairing are the cowl flaps, shown here in the open position. The P-40 parts manuals referred to the radiator fairing as the bottom cowling. It housed two radiators for cooling the engine and one oil cooler.

The six exhaust ducts are clearly visible from this angle. Prominent features on the leading edges of the wing were bulged fairings that covered the upper parts of the main landing gear struts and the trunnions on which they pivoted. From those bulged fairings, extending to the rear on the bottoms of the wings were housings for the main-gear struts when retracted, with a door on each side of the housing.

The Curtiss P-40-CU was powered by the Allison V-1710-33 engine, and in this photograph, Army Air Corps mechanics are servicing one of these engines and its accessories. Above the cowling are the blast tubes for the two .50-caliber machine guns. *Stan Piet collection*

Ground crewmen push a P-40-CU of the 8th Pursuit Group into position on a hardstand at its home base at Langley Field, Virginia. This aircraft was marked number 103 on the dorsal fin. Note the absence of .50-caliber machine gun blast tubes above the cowling. *National Museum of the United States Air Force*

The P-40 numbered 97 and assigned to the 8th Pursuit Group had an indistinct insignia on the side of the fuselage and a white or possibly yellow nose. The nose color indicated the number of the squadron within the group, and usually these colors were white, yellow, red, and sometimes blue. *National Museum of the United States Air Force*

Curtiss P-40-CU, Army Air Corps serial number 39-288, is parked on a wooden hardstand, with a revetment visible to the far right. The aircraft's number, 45, appears in unusually large numbers on the cowling. The machine guns are not mounted, and the gun ports in the wings and the top of the cowling have been covered.

The same P-40-CU seen in the preceding photograph, serial number 39-288, is seen from the left rear. The tail number, 9288, is marked in on the dorsal fin. During the period covered in this book, Air Corps and, later, Army Air Forces tail numbers equated to the military serial number less the first digit. Thus, tail number 9288 referred to serial number 39-288.

Curtiss P-40-CU, US Army Air Corps serial number 39-173, assigned to the 35th Pursuit Squadron, 8th Pursuit Group, suffered damage, including a bent propeller, from a belly landing in 1941. On the side of the fuselage is the leaping black panther insignia of the 35th Pursuit Squadron. *National Museum of the United States Air Force*

CHAPTER 3
P-40A and P-40B

This aircraft, Air Corps serial number 40-326, was a dedicated reconnaissance plane designated P-40A. In this April 1941 photograph, it bears markings of the 31st Pursuit Group, and the access door on the side of the fuselage is open, allowing a glimpse of the Fairchild K-3B vertical reconnaissance camera with zippered, insulated cover. *National Museum of the United States Air Force*

At least two of the P-40-CU aircraft, 40-326 and 40-188, were modified to P-40A configuration, which was to include K-3B reconnaissance cameras, under orders from Gen. Hap Arnold. Further orders in mid-June 1941 directed that sixteen additional aircraft be similarly modified in order to equip the 1st Photo Group. Given the mediocre results of the initial conversion, it is uncertain how many, if any, of the second group were actually modified to photoreconnaissance standards.

After production of the H81A-1 (Tomahawk I) was completed, production of the P-40 for the US Army Air Corps resumed, with 324 units left on the initial 524-unit order. However, based on the lessons learned from combat, there were changes made to the design such that the new production aircraft bore the Curtiss model number H81A-2, and the military designation P-40B-CU.

The new model doubled the number of .30-caliber machine guns in each wing, to two, featured self-sealing fuel tanks, and added armor plate and bullet-resistant glass to the cockpit, all of which added weight. The propeller too was heavier, and was a Curtiss Electric unit with aluminum alloy blades rather then the steel-blade units used on earlier models. The result of all of this was an aircraft weighing 385 pounds more than its predecessor, with a resultant drop in top speed to 352 Mph.

In May 1941, the order was reduced to 131 aircraft, with the remaining 193 aircraft on the US order to be the more capable P-40C. However, a further 110 aircraft of the type were built for the Commonwealth, although the Royal Air Force (RAF) subsequently transferred a number of these to the Soviet Union. The type was known at the Tomahawk IIA.

The P-40B incorporated improvements over the P-40-CU to make the aircraft more combat-ready, including adding an extra .30-caliber machine gun to each wing. Armor was installed for the protection of the pilot, and self-sealing fuel tanks were included. These additions added 385 pounds over the P-40-CU, and the maximum speed, 352 miles per hour, was five less than that of the P-40-CU.

This P-40B at Hamilton Army Airfield, near Novato, California, has markings for aircraft number 11 of the 55th Pursuit Squadron, 35th Pursuit Group. On the side of the fuselage is the squadron insignia, featuring a crossed arrow and sword with small wings to the sides of their intersection. The number 11 is on the cowling and the dorsal fin. *National Museum of the United States Air Force*

This P-40B lacks any markings visible from this angle except for the national insignia. On the dorsal fin is a formation light with a white, teardrop-shaped lens. Unlike most US pursuit and fighter planes introduced in the late 1930s, the P-40s had smooth exterior surfaces due to the use of flush riveting. *National Museum of the United States Air Force*

A P-40B, numbered 41 of the 18th Pursuit Group, flies high above the Pacific around mid-1941. The 18th Pursuit Group was based at Wheeler Field, Oahu, Territory of Hawaii, at the time. Two-thirds of the aircraft at Wheeler Field on December 7, 1941, were destroyed or disabled during the Japanese attacks.

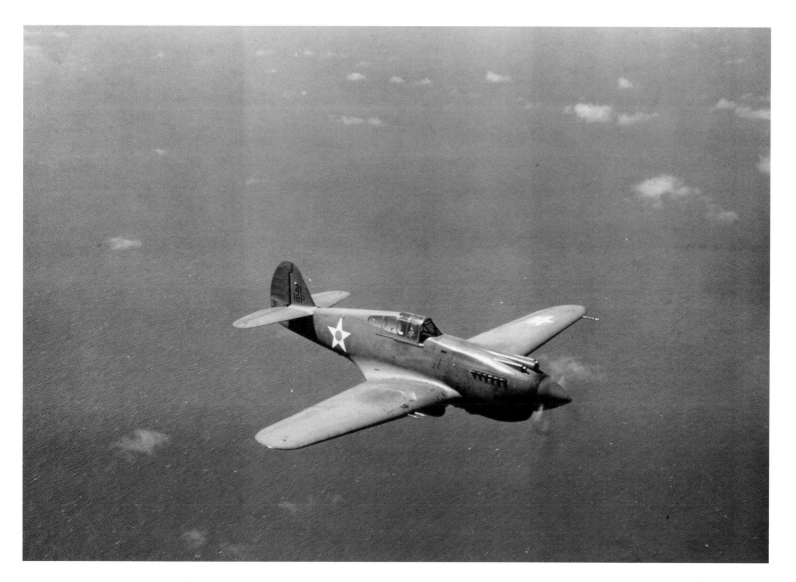

The same P-40B of the 18th Pursuit Group seen in the preceding photo is viewed from a more forward angle. The twin .30-caliber machine guns in the right wing are clearly visible. The long blast tubes for the .50-caliber machine guns seen in earlier photos of P-40s have been replaced by short blast tubes.

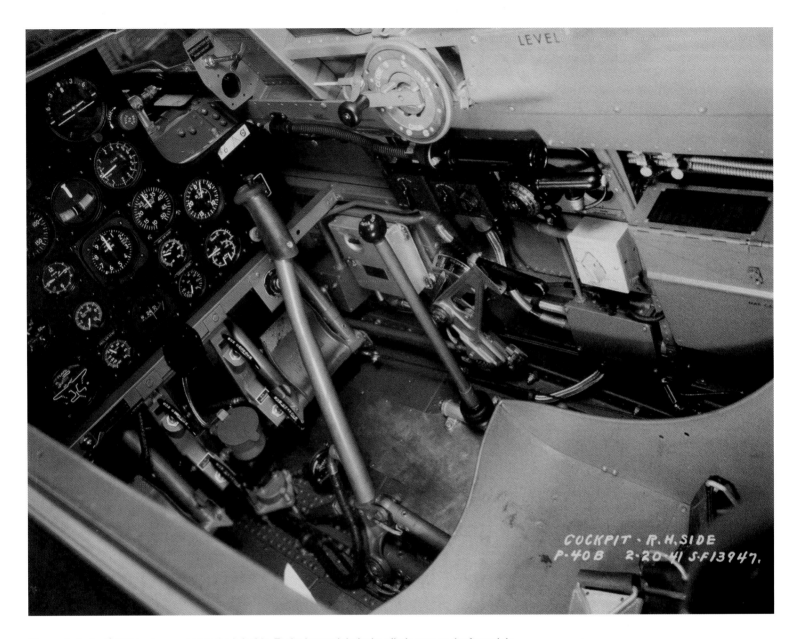

The cockpit of a P-40B is observed from the left side. To the lower right is the pilot's seat, to the front right of which is the emergency manual hydraulic pump handle. To the front of the seat is the flight control stick and the rudder pedals. The upper corners of the instrument panel were cut out to accommodate the rears of the .50-caliber machine guns, which are dismounted in this photo. At the top center of the photo is the canopy-operating crank. *National Museum of the United States Air Force*

CHAPTER 4
P-40C

Although very similar in appearance to the preceding types of P-40s, the P-40C differed in several respects, including the addition of a mounting rack and sway braces for a fifty-two-gallon external auxiliary fuel tank, as seen in this photo of a P-40C marked with the number 20 on the dorsal fin. Kits also were provided for adding the racks and auxiliary tanks to P-40Bs. This P-40C, aircraft number 20 of the 33rd Pursuit Squadron, 8th Pursuit Group, photographed in Iceland in the autumn of 1941, is tied down to concrete weights to prevent wind damage. *National Museum of the United States Air Force*

The final group of 193 aircraft from the original USAAC order were delivered as P-40Cs. The P-40C differed from the P-40B in that the type of self-sealing fuel tank was changed, and the aircraft was equipped to utilize a fifty-two-gallon centerline drop tank.

Production of the P-40C, which was carried out under contract AC-15802, began in March 1941, and ended in May of the same year.

While production of the P-40C was modest and its US use limited, that was not the case for the export version, the Tomahawk IIB, of which 930 were produced. The Tomahawk IIB was ordered by the British, and most were used by Commonwealth Air Forces,

including the Royal Egyptian Air Force, the South African Air Force, the Royal Australian Air Force, and of course the RAF.

In addition to flying the Tomahawk IIB, the British also transferred some of the type to Allied nations, including 194 transferred to the Soviet Union (along with ten USAAF P-40Cs), forty-two to the Turkish Air Force, and most notably China.

One hundred of the aircraft on the British order were diverted to fill an order from the Chinese Aircraft Manufacturing Company (CAMCO). These were to be the initial aircraft of the American Volunteer Group (AVG), the famed Flying Tigers.

Curtiss P-40C Warhawks of the 33rd Pursuit Squadron are parked at an airfield near Reykjavik, Iceland, in 1941. They had arrived offshore on the carrier USS *Wasp* on August 6 of that year and had flown from that ship to the base, replacing a RAF squadron that had been assisting in the defense of Iceland.
National Museum of the United States Air Force

Curtiss P-40C, US Army Air Force (USAAF) serial number 41-13429, suffered a rough landing and a bent propeller at a very snowy 2nd Service Group airfield in Iceland on February 6, 1943. About a year earlier, the red circle at the center of the national insignia had been officially deleted. Note the light color, likely a squadron color, on the front half of the propeller spinner. An extremely faint aircraft number, 132, is painted in a dark color on the cowling and in a lighter color, possibly gray or yellow, on the dorsal fin.
National Museum of the United States Air Force

Although several P-40 pilots managed to take off during the December 7, 1941, Japanese attacks on US military installations on Oahu, many P-40s were caught on the ground and damaged or destroyed. This example was damaged beyond repair in front of Hangar No.4 at Wheeler Field. Most of the fuselage and empennage have burned to cinders, and the pilot's seat is lying in the wreckage of the cockpit.

This Warhawk, plane number 62 of the 18th Pursuit Group, was damaged during the Japanese attack on Wheeler Field and is sitting on a wooden stand awaiting repair. Before the commencement of the attack on December 7, 1941, the 18th Pursuit Group had forty-six P-40Bs and eight P-40Cs that were in flying condition at Wheeler Field. On the fixed rear panel of the canopy are two round openings; these provided access for the fuselage fuel tank filler (front) and the oil tank filler (rear).

Curtiss P-40C, USAAF serial number 41-13468, of the 31st Fighter Squadron is parked underneath camouflage netting at an air base in the Caribbean in December 1942. The plane number, 91, is barely visible on the forward part of the cowling. Inside the windshield is an armor-glass panel, which protected the pilot's head from frontal fire. This Warhawk crashed on April 7, 1943, in the mountains north of La Hoya, Panama. *National Museum of the United States Air Force*

The British operated a version of the P-40C that they designated the Tomahawk IIB, receiving 775 of them from November 1940 to August 1941. Many of them served in the North African campaign and were especially valuable in the ground-attack and close-support roles. Here, RAF pilots scramble to man their Tomahawks at a desert base. Underneath the horizontal stabilizer of the second plane is the RAF serial number, AN3– (the last two digits are indistinct), consistent with that of a Tomahawk IIB. *National Museum of the United States Air Force*

CHAPTER 5
P-40D

The P-40D marked a significant change in the profile of the front of the Warhawks. The instigation for this change was the new engine, the Allison V-1710-39. Because this engine's output shaft was several inches higher than that of the V-1710-33, a cowling with less of a down-slope at the upper front was designed, which also necessitated a larger propeller spinner.

Creation of the P-40D was directly related to a failed effort to develop a successor to the P-40, the Curtiss XP-46. The XP-46 was powered by the Allison V-1710-39, which drove the propeller through a gearbox with a raised output shaft. The output shaft of the -33 model used in the P-40B and P-40C had been through a long nose case with internal spur reduction gearing (not elliptical gears as some sources state), with the result being that the output shaft was more centrally located relative to the block.

While the change in engine design meant a redesign to the aircraft cowl, the new gearbox was substantially more reliable than the old one. The arrangement of the new engine meant that the cowl-mounted .50 caliber machine guns were no longer practical. To offset this loss, the two wing-mounted .30-caliber machine guns found on the P-40C were replaced with a pair of .50-caliber machine guns in each wing. The considerably larger size of the .50-caliber guns required a redesign of the gun mountings and ammunition stowage.

A further result of the elimination of the cowl-mounted guns was a redesign of the instrument panel. This unusual side effect stemmed from the previous inverted - design panel being so arranged in order provide clearance for the receivers of the guns, which had protruded into the panel.

Further changes to the cockpit were made in order to increase visibility and protection for the pilot. A section of bulletproof glass was added in front of the pilot, the rear windows were enlarged, and 111 pounds of armor plate guarded the pilot.

So extensive were the changes to the airframe that Curtiss assigned it a new model number, the H87A-1. Only twenty-three P-40Ds were produced for the Army Air Corps before production for that agency switched to the more heavily armed P-40E. However, as with so many variants of the P-40, overseas exports of the type were substantially higher, with the RAF ordering 560 examples, which they dubbed Kittyhawk I. After twenty were delivered, a change order resulted in the balance of the type have six rather than four .50 caliber machine guns, mounted three per wing.

As a result of the redesign, the .50-caliber machine guns were removed from the cowling, and a larger bottom cowling was developed to house new radiators and oil cooler. Changes were instituted to the shapes of the canopy and the rear of the fuselage, and the four .30-caliber machine guns in the wings were replaced by four .50-caliber machine guns.

Although information is lacking on this photograph of P-40 Warhawks at an air base, it likely was taken during or in preparation for one of the massive US Army maneuvers in 1941, either in Louisiana or in the Carolinas. Aircraft participating in those maneuvers were marked with various symbols indicating which forces they were part of, and those symbols included white crosses. Some of these planes may have included the recently introduced P-40Ds, of which a total of only twenty-three were produced. *National Museum of the United States Air Force*

This P-40D displays the enlarged propeller spinner and bottom cowling and the new, oblong instead of round opening at the front of the carburetor air scoop. The four .50-caliber machine guns standard for the P-40D have not been installed in the wings. Note the six tapered engine-exhaust stacks. *National Museum of the United States Air Force*

Although this photograph did not come with identification, this plane is presumed to be a P-40D and may be the same one shown in the preceding photograph. In February 1941, the Army Air Corps issued a directive eliminating the national insignia from the top of the right wing and the bottom of the left wing. *National Museum of the United States Air Force*

While the US Army Air Forces ordered only twenty-three P-40Ds, the British contracted for 560 planes based on the P-40D, which they designated the Kittyhawk I. Although the first twenty Kittyhawk Is were armed with four wing-mounted .50-caliber machine guns, subsequent planes were delivered with six wing-mounted .50s. Seen here is the first Kittyhawk I, RAF serial number AK571, which lacked machine guns. *Stan Piet collection*

INSTRUMENT PANEL

The P-40D instrument panel varied from that of preceding models of the Warhawk in that it lacked cutouts at the upper corners for the breech ends of .50-caliber machine guns because those guns had been eliminated from the fuselage. There were significant differences in the contents of the P-40D instrument panel and those of earlier models of the Warhawk. There was a cutout at the top center of the P-40D instrument panel to accommodate the gun sight. *National Museum of the United States Air Force*

The Curtiss P-40E was very similar to the P-40D with the exception of the addition of two .50-caliber machine guns, resulting in three .50s in each wing. This up-gunning of the Warhawk was based on a British decision to add two extra machine guns to their Kittyhawk Is, and because of the US Army's preference for the increased firepower, it cancelled the P-40D project after only twenty-three were built. Seen here is P-40E-1-CU 41-36504.

The US Army Air Corps also opted to move to the three .50-caliber machine guns per wing arrangement. This change, as well as relocating the carburetor air scoop six inches forward, along with a few minor changes, resulted in the creation of the P-40E, or Curtiss H87A-2. The first flight of this variant took place in August 1941.

The USAAC purchased 2,320 P-40E aircraft in two groups. The first group of 820 aircraft was designated P-40E-CU, while the second group of 1,500 fighters was designated P-40E-1-CU. The second group of aircraft included provisions for carrying three small bombs under each wing. Many of the aircraft from the second group were turned over to the British under provisions of the Lend-Lease Act, which had been signed into law on March 11, 1941. Prior to passage of the Lend-Lease act, Curtiss aircraft for Allied use had been purchased outright by first the Anglo-French Purchasing Board, and later by the British Direct Purchase Commission. In British service the P-40E was known as the Kittyhawk IA.

On the leading edge of the left wing of this P-40E, the three .50-caliber machine gun muzzles are slightly recessed. There was another configuration of the guns on P-40Es where the barrels protruded slightly in advance of the leading edges of the wings.

This P-40E is likely the same one seen in the preceding photograph. The filler tubes for the fuselage fuel tank and the oil tank that were protruding through the left rear side panel of the cockpit canopy of preceding models of the P-40 had been deleted.

A P-40E is seen from the front, providing a good idea of the location and spacing of the .50-caliber machine gun ports in the leading edges of the wings. Note the design of the airflow dividers in the front of the bottom cowling, which had been changed to this configuration starting with the P-40D.

As seen in this photo of a P-40E from the left rear, the absence on the top cowl of fairings for .50-caliber machine guns is most apparent. The control surfaces of the P-40s were of aluminum frames with fabric covering. The skin of the aircraft was of Alclad, on a framework of aluminum-alloy stringers, shear beams, and bulkheads.

At the Curtiss-Wright Airplane Division plant in Buffalo, New York, the tail of a new P-40E has been hoisted to allow the man in the cockpit to perform a ground gunnery test. The plane bears a prewar US national insignia and a British-style camouflage scheme with two upper colors and a lighter color on the undersides. *National Museum of the United States Air Force*

This P-40E of the 20th Pursuit Group apparently is wearing markings for 1941 war game maneuvers, consisting of a large, roughly painted, light-colored circle around the national insignia on the fuselage, and a similar circle but separate from the national insignia on the bottom of the wing. A squadron color is painted on the front of the cowling. *National Museum of the United States Air Force*

Rows of P-40Es are lined up at an air base during the Louisiana or Carolina Maneuvers in 1941. They are marked with temporary white crosses to indicate the force they are part of. These planes are unarmed; the single P-40E facing the camera in the right background has what appears to be three pieces of tape over the apertures for the machine gun barrels on each wing. *National Museum of the United States Air Force*

A US Army Air Force P-40E-1-CU Warhawk, USAAF serial number 41-25009, is being loaded on board the aircraft carrier USS *Ranger* (CV-4) on April 15, 1942. The sides of the cowls have been removed for purposes of installing a hoisting sling; note the man in the cockpit holding the right cowl panel against the fuselage side. This is one of sixty-eight P-40Es bound for Accra, the Gold Coast (now Ghana), in Africa. On May 10, those Warhawks would fly off the deck of the *Ranger* for Accra. Large, roughly painted aircraft numbers were painted on the fuselages.

A good view is available of the underside of a USAAF P-40E being hoisted aboard USS *Ranger* on April 15, 1942. The national insignia still had the red circle at the center but this feature would be deleted a month later. The "US Army" markings on the undersides of the wings also would soon be discontinued. Note the machine-gun access panels outboard of the wheel wells, with spent-casing and link ejector chutes and, to the rears, bulges to give clearance for the breech ends of the guns.

A P-40E is being triced-up (navy terminology for hauled up and secured) to save space on the hangar deck of USS *Ranger* on April 14, 1942. The main landing gear wheels are resting in slings, and cable slings are fastened to the aft part of the fuselage.

American and British military personnel survey the remains of a P-40E after it crashed into a garden, killing the pilot, around the latter part of 1943. In the background are a wrecker and a tractor/semi-trailer, standing by until called in to remove the wreckage.

This view of P-40E-1-CU, USAAF serial number 41-24967, reportedly was taken while the plane was being used for training purposes in the southern United States in 1942. It was painted in British-style camouflage. Note the ring and bead sights on top of the cowling.

This survivor which was painted to replicate a P-40E, tail number 11456, served with the Royal Canadian Air Force from 1941–46. It had a varied postwar career, at one point being displayed on the roof of a gas station in Everett, Washington. After restoration and several years of air show performance the aircraft and pilot Robert Baranaskas were lost in a fatal crash into the Atlantic on April 5, 2009. *Rich Kolasa*

The plane has been refinished in a USAAF camouflage scheme of Olive Drab over Neutral Gray. It wears a tail number replicating that of P-40E-1-CU serial number 41-1456, and has the type of national insignia that was authorized through May 1942. *Rich Kolasa*

The exhaust stubs on this Warhawk are the flattened, "fishtail" type that was introduced partway into P-40E production. This design had the benefit of dampening flames, which the earlier type of exhaust lacked, often giving away the position of the plane during nighttime operations. *Author's photo*

The front of the intake of the bottom cowling is viewed. It is divided to direct the airflow to the two radiators to the sides and the oil cooler at the bottom. Details of the main landing gear oleo struts also are visible, including the data plates affixed to the front of them. *Author's photo*

Shark's mouth and eyes nose art of the type popularized by the Flying Tigers in China adorn this Warhawk. The cowl flaps are open at the rear of the bottom cowling. Projecting from the leading edge of the wing is the pitot tube. *Author's photo*

The landing-gear doors were mounted on piano hinges. These doors were connected by drag links to the oleo struts, and the action of the struts lowering or retracting caused the doors to open and shut. Covers are fitted to the main landing gear wheels, fastened with four slotted screws. *Author's photo*

The left main landing gear is viewed from the front. Running along the inboard side of the oleo strut is the hydraulic brake line. The data plate on the strut includes its serial number, servicing information, and warnings. The dome-shaped front of the landing-gear fairing provided a cover for the trunnion of the oleo strut. *Author's photo*

The inboard side of the right main landing gear is depicted. The silver-colored part of the oleo strut is part of the piston of the oil and pneumatic shock absorber that is an integral part of the strut. To the rear of the piston is the torsion link, the scissors-like fitting that transmits torsional force from the axle at the bottom of the strut to the strut. *Author's photo*

The tail wheel and strut are seen from the right side. The strut was operated by a hydraulic retracting cylinder inside the fuselage. In the bay to the front of the strut, part of the boot that keeps foreign objects and mud out of the bay is visible. *Author's photo*

The upper part of the left main landing gear is viewed from the rear, with the open cowl flaps to the bottom right. Retracting links attached to each side of the oleo strut operated the strut. To the right of the right strut is a fixed, toothed gear, which engaged a pinion on the upper part of the oleo strut. Because the oleo strut was designed to swivel in its trunnion, the movement of the pinion against the fixed gear when the strut was being retracted caused it to rotate ninety degrees so the wheel fit flat into the wheel well. The process was reversed when the main landing gear was lowered. *Author's photo*

The right horizontal stabilizer and elevator are shown, along with the lower part of the rudder. The stabilizer was formed of an Alclad skin over aluminum-alloy frame, while the elevator was made of doped fabric over an aluminum-alloy frame. A trim tab is at the rear of the elevator. *Author's photo*

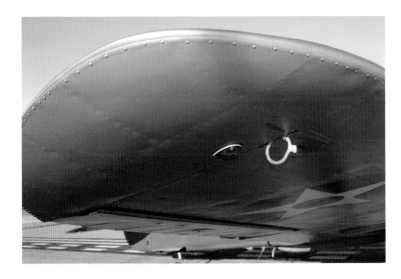

The underside of the right wing of the Warhawk is viewed from below the wingtip facing aft. A navigation light with a green, teardrop-shaped lens is on the wingtip panel. A similar one is on the top of the panel. Also in view is a spring-loaded tie-down ring which can be pushed up into the wing when not in use. Note the raised rivets on the edge of the wing and the flush rivets elsewhere. *Author's photo*

Above the pilot's seat is a large, cushioned headrest. The bulkhead the headrest was mounted on was armor plate, part of the protective armor for the pilot. Also, in addition to the armor glass in the windshield, there was a steel armor plate below the armor glass. *Author's photo*

In a view of the cockpit canopy from the right side, the steel cable that operates the sliding canopy is visible inside the track. Starting with the P-40D, the windshield assembly was redesigned and now featured a flat plate of ballistic glass at the front. Behind the windshield is the gun sight. *Author's photo*

A view of the underside of a P-40E gives an excellent idea of the appearance of the main landing gear when retracted, as well as the landing-gear doors in the closed positions. Also in view is an auxiliary fuel tank. To the rear of the inboard side of the right wing flap is an identification light with a clear lens. *Author's photo*

CHAPTER 7
P-40F

Because of their lack of turbosuperchargers, the Warhawks up through the P-40E performed poorly at high altitudes, severely limiting their usefulness as fighter aircraft. To remedy this situation, the British Rolls-Royce Merlin engine with a single-stage, two-speed turbosupercharger was mated to the Warhawk, resulting in the P-40F model, or, in British service, the Kittyhawk II. These engines were produced under license to Packard in Warren, Ohio, and were designated the Packard Merlin V-1650-1. This P-40F was photographed on February 22, 1942. *National Museum of the United States Air Force*

Except for the Allison V-1710B which was designed for use in Navy airships, all V-1710 engines were equipped with engine-driven geared turbosuperchargers. However, the factory-installed supercharger was a single-stage unit. Allison engineers designed the engines to accommodate turbosupercharging as well, but turbosuperchargers were not installed on the H81 aircraft, nor were they installed on the P-40D or E. Because of that, the performance of these aircraft at high altitudes was severely lacking.

In a somewhat long way around to increase P-40 altitude performance, rather than applying a two-stage supercharger or a turbosupercharger to the Allison, the decision was made instead to adapt the airframe to use the Rolls-Royce Merlin 28, which was equipped with a two-speed supercharger.

The first aircraft so equipped was a modified P-40D, serial number 40-360. The modified aircraft, which was redesignated XP-40F, flew for the first time on June 30, 1941. Performance at altitude showed marked improvement with the Merlin powerplant, so the P-40F was ordered into production. The production aircraft used the Packard-built, Rolls-Royce-licensed V-1650-1 Merlin. To accommodate the new engine, the nose of the aircraft was

redesigned yet again. Carburetor air was now drawn from the chin scoop, rather than from the atop-cowl scoop used on the previous Allison-powered aircraft. The scoop itself was redesigned as well, in order to accommodate the Merlin's radiators.

Production of the new type, designated P-40F-CU, began in January 1942. This production block included ninety-six aircraft, plus a single YP-40F, serial number 41-13602, and was followed by a block of 603 P-40F-1-CU aircraft.

A problem soon surfaced with the Merlin-powered aircraft in the form of poor directional stability, a fault blamed on the increased horsepower of the Merlin. After some experimentation with dorsal fillets, the final solution was found to be lengthening the rear fuselage by twenty inches. This change was introduced at the beginning of the P-40F-5-CU production block, which numbered 123 aircraft. Successive production blocks included much less drastic changes, such as manually operated cowl flaps (block -10 aircraft, 177 units), winterization (block -15 aircraft, 200 units) and upgraded electrical and oxygen systems (block -20 aircraft, 112 units).

The RAF were supplied 150 of the short-tail P-40F aircraft, designating them Kittyhawk II, but twenty-one were lost *en route*.

A P-40F peels off from a formation of Warhawks assigned to the Army Air Forces Advanced Training School at Moore Field, Mission, Texas. Note the mottled paint on the nearest aircraft. The two top planes are P-40F-1-CUs, USAAF serial numbers 41-14180 and 41-14181. With the P-40F, the carburetor air scoop on top of the cowling was deleted; the carburetor air intake had been relocated to the chin scoop.

The layout of the P-40F cockpit and instrument panel are depicted. The floor was the top of the wing assembly, mounted on which are the control stick and the emergency manual hydraulic pump handle. At the top of the instrument panel is a cutout for the gun sight, not mounted. Below the flight-instrument gauges are switches for various systems. To the left are the throttle and trim controls; to the right is the hand crank for operating the sliding canopy. At the bottom is the seat cushion. *National Museum of the United States Air Force*

This photograph, dated August 1, 1942, was taken to document the installation of an N-3A optical gun sight above the instrument panel. This gun sight was used on many US combat aircraft in the early 1940s and was a rather crude instrument but was cheap, adequate, and available in large quantities. *National Museum of the United States Air Force*

An N-3A optical gun sight with a sun screen installed in a P-40F cockpit is shown in a February 1942 photograph. This particular N-3A sight was manufactured by the Service Tool and Engineering Company of Dayton, Ohio. It was fitted with a U-shaped crash pad. Though this gun sight and the one in the preceding photo both were N-3As, they appear to be different; this is because there was great variation in the sight heads and the manner in which the sights were mounted. *National Museum of the United States Air Force*

In a pilot's-eye view of the instrument panel and gun sight of a P-40F, the airspeed indicator is to the left of the gun sight, which appears to be an N-3A. Note the long, vertical reticle at the center of the sight glass and the three short, horizontal reticles. A small placard on the instrument panel lists the radio call sign as 113601, which likely coincided with the tail number, in which case this plane was the second P-40F produced (41-13601). *National Museum of the United States Air Force*

On the upper panel of a P-40F instrument panel are flight and engine gauges, such as an altimeter, flap and wheel indicator, tachometer, manifold pressure gauge, coolant temperature indicator, engine gauge unit, flight indicator, and at the bottom center, a compass. Below the instrument panel is the main switch box, which contains switches for the bomb safety, gun camera, lights, compass, gun sight, and other systems, as well as circuit breakers for all systems. *National Museum of the United States Air Force*

On the left side of the cockpit of a P-40F, at the upper front is the throttle quadrant, including the propeller control, below which is the fuel selector. To the rear of the throttle quadrant are the rudder and elevator trim-tab controls; below these are the auxiliary tank and bomb-release controls. Next to the seat toward the left are the landing-gear control and the flap control. *National Museum of the United States Air Force*

One of the P-40F-CU Warhawks, USAAF serial number 41-13602, was used as a test plane for experiments with the cooling system and the rudder. Several different designs and locations for radiator housings were tried, including the one shown here. In another set of tests, the radiators were placed in enlarged wing roots. Reportedly, this plane was referred to unofficially as YP-40F. *National Museum of the United States Air Force*

A P-40F, as indicated by the lack of a carburetor intake over the cowling and the absence of a vent in the left side of the windshield assembly (a trait of the otherwise similar P-40L) is being prepped for starting the engine. Two ground crewmen are standing by with fire extinguishers in the event of an engine fire. The plane has a tiger's mouth but, interestingly, no national insignia under the right wing.

Warhawks are lined up at an unidentified airfield. The tail in the foreground belongs to P-40-CU USAAF serial number 39-210. The next two planes are P-40F-1-CUs, 41-14188 and 412-13712. Note the star decoration on the wheel cover of 41-14188 as well as the nickname *Joyce* and number 79 on the cowling.

During a mission to deliver P-40s to Accra on the west coast of Africa in July 1942, Cpl. R.J. Klein services the engine while 2nd Lt. R.W. Kimball paints a nickname starting with Ruey on the cowling of a P-40F-1-CU, USAAF serial number 41-13965. A stencil below the windshield identifies the pilot of this plane as R.W. Kimball. This was part of a group of planes bound for the Flying Tigers in China.

In a view of a P-40F-1-CU in flight, probably 41-13718 from what is visible of the tail number, another feature of the F model is prominent: the once-more revised bottom cowling, which was deeper than its predecessor and extended farther to the front, with the front of the cowling almost touching the propeller. Note that the tail wheel doors are not completely closed. *National Museum of the United States Air Force*

At Fighter Strip No.2 on Guadalcanal, P-40Fs are parked on the engine-maintenance line awaiting repairs. The plane with the shot-up left wing at the center, 41-19823, is a P-40F-15-CU, one of the F-model planes with lengthened fuselages that were issued starting with the P-40F-5-CU production block. To the right is a P-40 wing assembly and main landing gear with the fuselage removed. Although the tail number of the plane to the left is indistinct, the first three digits are 114, consistent with a P-40F-5-CU or P-40F-10-CU. *National Museum of the United States Air Force*

In this photograph taken at Fighter Strip No.2, Guadalcanal, two P-40Fs are undergoing engine changes. The engine has been removed from the airframe to the left, and a hoist sling has been attached to the Packard Rolls-Royce Merlin engine on the P-40F to the right. *National Museum of the United States Air Force*

In another view of the same two P-40Fs seen in the preceding photo, the original caption indicates that the engine is being removed from the plane to the left. A cargo truck with an A-frame boom is doing the heavy lifting and moving. The airframe to the right is awaiting an engine change. *National Museum of the United States Air Force*

In a final photo from Fighter Strip No.2 on Guadalcanal, mechanics work to get P-40Fs back into action. In the left background is a scrapyard, with various airplane carcasses and components lying in heaps. This and the preceding sequence of Guadalcanal photos were taken by Robert Gray of Curtiss-Wright's Service Department. *National Museum of the United States Air Force*

A Warhawk, apparently a P-40F judging from the lack of a carburetor intake above the cowling and the absence of a vent on the left side of the windscreen (a feature of the similarly appointed P-40L), has crash-landed at a desert location. Lying crumpled on the ground to the rear of the wing is the smashed auxiliary fuel tank and several sway braces. *National Museum of the United States Air Force*

CHAPTER 8
P-40G

The P-40G was not the next P-40 model following the P-40F, as the G suffix might suggest, but rather was the designation for forty-four P-40-CUs modified to improve their combat-worthiness. Modifications included the installation of Tomahawk IIA wings mounting a total of four .30-caliber machine guns, and the installation of self-sealing tanks and pilot armor. Seen here is Herb Fisher, Curtiss-Wright's chief test pilot, at the controls of a P-40G. Note the two sealed gun ports on the leading edge of the wing. *National Museum of the United States Air Force*

The P-40G was not a factory-produced version of the P-40, but nevertheless the USAAC records indicate the service owned forty-eight examples of the type. This is a result of the combination of rapidly evolving models of the P-40, plus the high number of ground loop incidents involving the P-40-CU. By early 1940, almost fifty of the 200 P-40-CUs purchased by the USAAC were out of service due to accidental wing damage. The Curtiss plant was by that time tooled for and producing the Tomahawk for the British Purchasing Commission. The decision was made to use the Tomahawk wing as a replacement for the out of production P-40-CU wing. However, the Tomahawk wing mounting was different, as were the gun mounts and ammo trays—requiring adapters for use in conjunction with the American fuselage and armament. Because even at this early date successive models of the P-40 through the P-40F had already been planned, the rebuilt hybrid aircraft were designated P-40Gs. The type, although intended as a training aircraft, saw limited service with the USAAC, although some were transferred to Russia.

A mechanic at an airfield at Oakland, California, is monitoring the refueling of a P-40G assigned to the 20th Pursuit Group in August 1941. Aft of the cockpit is a portrayal of a hand of cards: four sevens and an ace. The plane has the prewar style of national insignia on the wings but no insignia on the fuselage. *National Museum of the United States Air Force*

CHAPTER 9
P-40K

After the P-40F with its Packard/ Rolls-Royce Merlin engines, the next model of the Warhawk (discounting the P-40G, which was a modified P-40-CU) was the P-40K, which employed the Allison V-1710-74 engine. The V-1710-74 offered an additional 175 horsepower over the Allison V-1710-39 engine of the P-40E. Like the P-40F, the P-40K had short-fuselage and long-fuselage versions, with P-40K-1-CU and P-40K-5-CU production blocks having the shorter fuselage. Six .50-caliber machine guns were in the wings. *National Museum of the United States Air Force*

An Allison engine returned to the P-40 for the next type, the P-40K. This variant was powered by the Allison V-1710-73, which developed 1,325 horsepower, a 175 horsepower improvement over the V-1710-39 found in the P-40E. The -73 also lacked the gun synchronizer drives, which were no longer needed due to the earlier relocation of the guns to the wings rather than cowl.

The initial order of 600 P-40K aircraft were for the Chinese through Lend-Lease. However, after the Japanese attack on Pearl Harbor, the aircraft were instead initially retained by the USAAC, but soon the decision was made to transfer 340 to the RAF, and the number of P-40K on order was increased to 1,300 on June 15, 1942.

Initially the P-40K featured the so-called short fuselage, but it was found to have the same stability issues as the short P-40F. The initial corrective action attempted was the use of a dorsal

fillet. However, beginning with the -10-CU block the fuselage was lengthened by twenty inches, as it had been on the late P-40F type.

While widely used by the United States, a number of P-40Ks were supplied to Allied nations, although ironically, none went to China, for whom the type was originally intended. In Commonwealth service, the P-40K was known as the Kittyhawk III. In addition to the RAF, the Kittyhawk III saw service with the RNZAF and RAAF, while the Royal Canadian Air Force (RCAF) received nine P-40K-1-CU from the USAF. Other users included South Africa, Brazil (31 aircraft), and Russia (313 aircraft).

The Royal Air Force ordered a total of 364 P-40Ks and P-40Ms, designating them the Kittyhawk III. This example, photographed in July 1942, is RAF serial number FR241. Short-fuselage examples of the P-40K and Kittyhawk III had a noticeable fillet at the bottom of the leading edge of the dorsal fin, to improve longitudinal stability. This feature was not present on long-fuselage planes. *National Museum of the United States Air Force*

The same Kittyhawk III, FR241, is seen from another angle at Curtiss-Wright's plant at Buffalo on July 9, 1942. There was a small, rear-view mirror housed in a fairing on the left side of the rear frame of the windshield. The plane was painted in RAF camouflage of Dark Earth and Mid Stone on the upper surfaces and Azure Blue on the underside. The nomenclature stencil below the windscreen lists this plane as a P-40K-1, USAAF serial number 42-45831. The K-1 production block was manufactured between May and August 1942. *National Museum of the United States Air Force*

Sergeant Elmer J. Pence applies the final touches to a kill marking for a Japanese aircraft on P-40K-5-CU 42-9768, assigned to the 26th Fighter Squadron, 51st Fighter Group, in China. On the cowling is a mascot monkey on a chain. Clear views are available of the rear-view mirror on the windscreen frame and the round, red filler cap for the fuselage fuel tank below the sliding canopy. *National Museum of the United States Air Force*

On May 14, 1943, 1st Lt. John B. Griffith was flying this short-fuselage P-40K, nicknamed *Vera*, over New Guinea when the plane received some hits from a Japanese fighter plane, causing failure of the landing gear. He had to make a wheels-up landing at Dobodura Airfield, New Guinea, but was uninjured. Note the fillet at the base of the dorsal fin. *National Museum of the United States Air Force*

Warhawks covered with a blanket of snow are parked at Ladd Army Airfield, Fairbanks, Alaska Territory. The nearest plane is P-40K-5-CU 42-9835. These planes were painted in a tricolor camouflage scheme: two colors on the upper surfaces and another on the undersides of the aircraft. *National Museum of the United States Air Force*

Warhawks are lined up at the airport in Orlando, Florida, for a show in 1943. The first plane is P-40K-10-CU USAAF serial number 42-10121, a long-fuselage type. Note the presence of an antenna mast on the top deck to the rear of the sliding canopy; these masts appear to have been introduced to Warhawks starting with the P-40K, although they are sometime seen on P-40Fs, perhaps as a retrofit.

Curtiss P-40K-10-CU 42-9985 sports an unusual conglomeration of markings and decorations, from the shark's mouth and eyes on the front end to the multicolored vertical stripes and bands to the front and the rear, to the national insignia on the fuselage.

Curtiss P-40K-15-CU 42-10343 was a late-production K model, and from this angle, in a photograph taken on March 1, 1943, its long-type fuselage is evident. The longer fuselage was devised in an attempt to correct a longitudinal instability problem, which, according to Donovan Berlin, chief engineer of Curtiss-Wright and designer of the P-40, was due to the inefficient design of the bottom cowling and its contents, the radiators and oil cooler.

Curtiss P-40K-10-CU 42-10181 was converted to a two-seat, open-cockpit training aircraft designated TP-40K. This plane was not airworthy; rather, it was to instruct mechanics how to taxi the P-40. Because the plane was prone to nosing-over under certain conditions, a training wheel was installed on the front end to prevent such accidents. The TP-40K had dual controls and an intercom system. *National Museum of the United States Air Force*

In late May 1943, three members of Curtiss-Wright's Camp Curtissair, Buffalo, New York, inspect the training gear on the TP-40K. They are, left to right, S. S. Spaulding, Bob Mitchell, and Fred Lounsbury, and they designed the TP-40K. This airframe was intended to train ground crewmen at the camp, which was an Army Air Forces Technical Training Command Service School. *National Museum of the United States Air Force*

CHAPTER 10
P-40L

The P-40L was an attempt at a lightened version of the Warhawk, which had grown increasingly heavy with its armor, weapons, and protected fuel tanks. This reduction in weight was achieved by eliminating two of the wing machine guns, cutting down on the pilot's armor, and reducing the internal fuel capacity by thirty-seven gallons. The first fifty P-40Ls had the short fuselage; later ones had the long fuselage. The plane was powered by the Packard/Rolls-Royce Merlin V-1650-1 turbosupercharged engine. Shown here is P-40L-20-CU 42-11125, the fourth-from-last P-40L. *National Museum of the United States Air Force*

Still seeking to improve performance, with the P-40L a new strategy was employed by Curtiss—weight reduction. This was achieved by reducing the number of heavy .50-caliber machine guns from six to four, cutting the number of rounds per gun, reducing the amount of armor plate, and reducing fuel capacity—although all these changes were not made simultaneously.

The Packard Merlin V-1650-1 was again selected as the powerplant, with the cowl configured accordingly.

Production of the new type began with the P-40L-1-CU in January 1943. The fifty aircraft of this block had six .50-caliber machine guns, a full 157-gallon fuel capacity and short fuselages. Subsequent P-40L fighters had the long fuselage, including the next group, which were 220 P-40L-5-CU aircraft, featuring four .50-caliber guns and 120-gallon fuel capacity. The block 5 aircraft were produced in January–February 1943. During February and

March, 148 P-40L-10-CU aircraft were assembled; these lacked armor around the engine coolant tank but incorporated improved engine controls and electric trim tab actuation.

Modified identification lighting and a permanently mounted engine air filter were features of the 112 P-40L-15-CU aircraft assembled in March and April 1943.

The final production block of the type was 170 P-40L-20-CU, which incorporated improved radio and electrical systems and provisions for a self-destruct incendiary grenade.

A limited number of P-40L aircraft were powered by Allison V-1710 engines, and were redesignated P-40R-2-CU. These aircraft were used for training purposes.

The USAAF used the P-40L in the Mediterranean, and 100 of the type were supplied to the RAF, who designated them Kittyhawk II, a name they shared with the P-40F.

Curtiss P-40L-20-CU 42-11061 rests on a hardstand at Luke Field, Arizona. P-40s used for training at Luke Field had large codes on the fuselages with an X prefix and three numbers. These codes were on the cowling and on the fuselage aft of the cockpit. On the side of the windscreen is an extra vertical frame member, part of a ventilating panel. This panel is an important identifying feature for distinguishing between the P-40L and the long-fuselage P-40F. *National Museum of the United States Air Force*

A shipment of P-40Ls is being transported to North Africa in early 1943. At the lower right is the tail of P-40L-5-CU 42-10578, with a wavy camouflage-paint treatment around the edges of the empennage. To the far right is P-40L-5-CU 42-10500, and also visible are P-40L-5-CUs 42-10464 and 42-10596. A variety of camouflage schemes are on these planes, and they had US flags on the fuselages. Protective material is on the clear panels of the canopies. *National Museum of the United States Air Force*

The P-40M had several keynote features: an Allison V-1710-81 engine rated at 1,200 horsepower; a carburetor intake on top of the cowling; a perforated grille to the front of the engine exhausts on each side of the cowling, for taking in carburetor bypass air; reinforced ailerons; and the long fuselage. Shown here is P-40M-10-CU 43-5810. *National Museum of the United States Air Force*

The P-40M was a further development of the Allison-powered P-40L, and bears considerable resemblance to the P-40L-20-CU. The P-40M was powered by the Allison V-1710-81, which featured automatic boost control and was rated at 1,200 horsepower at takeoff. All 600 of the P-40M aircraft were built with the so-called long fuselage. Like the P-40L-20-CU, a fifteen-hole grille was on either side of the cowl just ahead of the exhaust stacks. These grilles allowed carburetor bypass air to enter through metal filters.

The first sixty aircraft of the type were included in production block P-40M-1-CU. This was followed by block P-40M-5-CU, which comprised 260 aircraft featuring permanent carburetor air cleaners and improved ailerons. The final block, the -15-CU, added mechanical landing gear indicators on the top of each wing. All were armed with six .50-caliber machine guns and had an internal fuel capacity of 157 gallons.

A small number of these aircraft were converted into two-seat trainer configuration and designated TP-40M.

While 336 of these aircraft were supplied to Allies under Lend-Lease, notably to the Commonwealth who classified them as Kittyhawk III, the USAAF retained, at least initially, 264 of the type. The USAAF used the aircraft as stateside trainers, as well as combat aircraft issued to the 51st Fighter Group in the China–Burma–India Theater, the 23rd Fighter Group in China, and the 18th in Guadalcanal, New Caledonia and New Guinea.

Other nations receiving P-40M included Brazil, Finland, New Zealand, and the Soviet Union, the latter getting fifty ex-USAAF P-40M as well as 170 ex-RAF Kittyhawk IIIs.

Curtiss P-40s and North American B-25 medium bombers share space at a maintenance area at an unidentified airfield. The nearest Warhawk, P-40M-1-CU 43-5460, is undergoing engine work. With the cowling removed, the carburetor-air bypass filter to the front of the engine exhausts is visible inside the light-colored rectangular frame. Air passed through the perforated grill in the cowling into the filter. Below the Allison engine are the radiators and oil cooler. Just beyond this plane is a P-40K-5-CU, USAAF serial number 42-97– (the last two digits of the tail number are illegible). *National Museum of the United States Air Force*

Lt. David M. Crum of the 344th Fighter Squadron, 343rd Fighter Group, the pilot of *Betty Jo*, P-40M-5-CU USAAF serial number 43-5715, made a belly landing in the Aleutians on October 12, 1944. The plane's nickname is visible below the engine exhausts. The national insignia is the style authorized in August 1943. *National Museum of the United States Air Force*

Curtiss P-40M-5-CU 43-5487 was converted to a two-seat trainer designated a TP-40M by cutting down the fuselage to the rear of the cockpit and adding a rear cockpit and canopy for the instructor. The plane was not armed, and it lacks the perforated grille to the front of the engine exhausts typically associated with the P-40M. The nose art is a likeness of a dachshund with *SHORT-SNORTER* written above it. In this photo taken over Florida, a USAAF instructor in the back seat is giving a lesson to a Brazilian Air Force student in the front seat.

Although documentation on the identity of this Warhawk-based trainer is not available, it appears to be a TP-40M, similar to the plane in the preceding photo. In the rear cockpit, the instructor, a Col. Dennison, gives a last-minute briefing to the student, a Brazilian Air Force pilot, before starting the engine.

The P-40N was another attempt to lighten the Warhawk to improve its performance, including such measures as omitting the battery and two of the .50-caliber machine guns, reducing the ammunition storage, and manufacturing the radiators and oil coolers from aluminum. Planes of the first production block, as seen in this photograph, looked much like the P-40M, including the same perforated grilles on each side of the cowling. However, the two machine guns per wing give this aircraft away as something other than a P-40M. *National Museum of the United States Air Force*

The last version of the P-40 to be mass-produced was the P-40N. Like the P-40M, the P-40N was powered by an Allison V-1710-81, but followed the pattern of the P-40L in regard to efforts to reduce weight, chiefly by reducing armament and fuel and ammunition capacity.

The first production block, 400 aircraft of the P-40N-1-CU model, was armed with four .50-caliber machine guns and had a 120 gallon fuel capacity. Further reducing weight was the use of aluminum rather than brass radiators, magnesium main landing gear wheels and, at least initially, eliminating the starting battery. The latter meant that these aircraft relied on external power for starting, a situation that was deemed unacceptable so the aircraft were modified to carry a battery. As a result of these weight savings, the P-40N-1-CU had a top speed of 378 miles per hour, besting all the other production P-40s.

A redesigned canopy that eliminated most of the framework found on earlier models was the hallmark of the -5-CU production block, which included 1,100 aircraft. At the same time the pilot's seat was redesigned and SCR-696 radio equipment began to be used.

The 100 aircraft of the -10-CU block were winterized and included a rate of climb indicator for the pilot.

By the time production of the 377 aircraft of the P-40N-15-CU began the value of six machine gun armament was recognized, and such armament was returned, despite the increase in weight.

The P-40N-20-CU, of which 1,523 were produced, boasted a 1,360 horsepower Allison V-1710-99 engine, and included provisions for triple tube rocket launchers, 500-pound bombs, or drop tanks under each wing.

The 500 aircraft each of the -25, -30, and -35 production blocks had little external variation from the -20, but the -30 incorporated non-metal self-sealing fuel tanks and revised instruments, while the -35 had improved radio and navigation gear.

One thousand examples of the P-40N-40-CU were ordered, although only 220 were actually built before production ceased in November 1944. These aircraft included all of the previous improvements to the P-40N, plus were powered by the V-1710-115, developing 1,200 horsepower and featuring automatic boost and propeller controls.

About thirty P-40Ns were modified into two-seat trainers by Curtiss. These aircraft were designated TP-40N.

Curtiss P-40N-1-CU USAAF serial number 42-104528 is an example of an N-model Warhawk from the first production block. With the next production block, the P-40N-5-CU, there would be a dramatic change in the canopy. The airframe was of the long-fuselage type.

The P-40N was by far the most-produced variant of the P-40, and was used not only by the USAAF, but Allied nations as well. The Soviets received 100 of the type, China 300, and Brazil forty-one. The Commonwealth took delivery of hundreds of the aircraft, dubbing them Kittyhawk IV. Kittyhawk IVs were operated by the RAF (456), Royal Australian Air Force (468), RCAF (35), and RNZAF (172). South Africa and The Netherlands also operated Kittyhawk IVs under Commonwealth control.

P-40N-1-CU USAAF serial number 42-104528 can be distinguished from a P-40M by the presence of two instead of three .50-caliber machine guns in each wing. A splotchy camouflage paint scheme was applied to the wings and the empennage. *National Museum of the United States Air Force*

Sue was the nickname of this P-40N-1-CU, USAAF serial number 42-104589, of the 51st Fighter Group. The plane is returning from a raid on a Japanese supply base at Kamaing, Burma, in 1943, having delivered a load of 500-pound bombs. A large number 1 is to the front of the national insignia, which at this point has white bars on the sides but without borders. Mottled camouflage paint is on the vertical tail. *National Museum of the United States Air Force*

An example of the second P-40N production block was USAAF serial number 42-104958, a P-40N-5-CU, as seen from the front. For every rule there is an exception, as exemplified by the six .50-caliber machine guns protruding through the leading edges of the wings, where P-40Ns technically were to have four machine guns until the fourth production block, when two more were added. *National Museum of the United States Air Force*

A side view of P-40N-5-CU 42-104958 shows the radically new canopy introduced with that production block. The sliding canopy frame was only around the perimeter of the assembly, making for greatly improved visibility. A large canopy to the rear of the sliding canopy replaced the semi-elliptical rear windows of earlier P-40s. Inside of that rear canopy, the upper deck of the fuselage had been radically remodeled, with an angled section coming down from the top rear to the bottom front of that canopy. *National Museum of the United States Air Force*

As part of the third production block of N-model Warhawks, P-40N-10-CU 42-106019 had the new style of canopy. The one hundred examples of this production block were completed in August 1943. The engine for the P-40Ns through the fourth production block was the Allison V-1710-81. *National Museum of the United States Air Force*

This P-40N-20-CU, USAAF serial number 43-23388, photographed in late 1943, was part of the most numerous production block of the P-40N, with 1,523 examples being completed during the period from September to December 1943. Aft of the antenna mast is a radio direction-finder (RDF) loop antenna. A pylon for a small bomb is under the wing. *National Museum of the United States Air Force*

A Brazilian Air Force pilot was at the controls of this P-40N-20-CU over Florida during World War II. He was part of a cadre receiving training in the latest aerial combat tactics at the Army Air Forces Tactical Center (AAFTAC) at Orlando. Adjacent to the national insignia on the fuselage were, front to rear, red, blue, white, and yellow stripes, and the spinner had red, blue, white, and yellow bands. *National Museum of the United States Air Force*

Starting with the P-40N-25-CU, self-sealing fuel tanks were installed. This bare-aluminum example, P-40N-25-CU 43-24380, was assigned to the 398th Fighter Squadron, 369th Fighter Group, a training unit based in the United States during World War II. The insignia of the 369th is on the top cowling; it depicts a flying vulture. *National Museum of the United States Air Force*

On November 22, 1944, the 15,000th fighter plane produced by Curtiss-Wright left the assembly line in Buffalo. It was a P-40N, and to commemorate the occasion, it was covered with a crazy quilt of markings, from a red spinner and a shark's mouth on the nose to the striped rudder, and in between, insignia of twenty-eight air forces with which Curtiss-built aircraft had served. In addition, there were 18 small Japanese flags and 20½ small German flags symbolizing the kills of the two highest-scoring P-40 aces, Wing Cdr. Clive "Killer" Caldwell of the Royal Australian Air Force, and Col. David Lee "Tex" Hill of the US Army Air Forces.

Curtiss P-40Ns of the 35th Fighter Squadron, 8th Fighter Group, are lined up at the airfield at Cape Gloucester, New Britain, in early February 1944. In the foreground is P-40N-5-CU 42-105288. Later that year, the 35th Fighter Squadron would replace its P-40Ns with Lockheed P-38 Lightnings. *National Museum of the United States Air Force*

The tail has been destroyed on this P-40N with markings for the Chinese Air Force. On the top of the fuselage aft of the radio-antenna mast is a radio direction-finder loop antenna. Hidden by the left wing is another P-40, with stripes on the rudder; the wrecked rudder on the aircraft in the foreground also shows evidence of stripes on its rudder. *National Museum of the United States Air Force*

Pilots scramble to their planes along a row of P-40Ns assigned to the Fourteenth Air Force in China. Although the original USAAF caption for the photo claims that the scramble was in response to an incoming Japanese air raid on the base, the men's smiles give the photo a posed appearance. *National Museum of the United States Air Force*

The number 55E on the cowling of this P-40N being prepared for a flight on November 19, 1943, is the freshest looking feature on this weather-beaten Warhawk. The first three digits of the tail number, 210, are discernible. The sway braces for a bomb or an auxiliary fuel tank under the belly of the plane are clearly visible.

Curtiss converted some 30 P-40Ns to TP-40N advanced trainers, featuring a rear cockpit and sliding canopy for the instructor and dual flight controls and instruments. The student sat in the forward cockpit. Above the front of the instructor's sliding canopy was a mirror, part of a periscopic system that enabled him to view to the front. *National Museum of the United States Air Force*

This TP-40N was based on the airframe of P-40N-30-CU USAAF serial number 44-7156. The forward sliding canopy was of different size and shape than the aft sliding canopy. Between the two sliding canopies was a fixed canopy with a horizontal frame member on each side. The mast antenna was moved aft from its normal position on the P-40N. *National Museum of the United States Air Force*

In order to make room for the second cockpit, the 68-gallon fuel tank was removed from the fuselage, leaving the aircraft with only a 54-gallon main wing tank plus a 35-gallon front wing fuel tank. Provisions for external fuel tanks were retained, however. *National Museum of the United States Air Force*

The same TP-40N seen in the preceding photos, USAAF serial number 44-7156, is shown parked on a tarmac, wheels chocked, and instructor and trainee in their cockpits. Because of the way the fuselage tapered to the rear of the front cockpit, it was necessary to install a fairing to the sides of the rear cockpit, to accommodate the shape of the bottom of the aft cockpit when closed.

Curtiss ceased producing P-40s in November 1944, six months before the end of World War II. Other fighter planes had long since supplanted the Warhawk, and, unlike the P-51, which enjoyed a combat career after World War II, the P-40s were relegated to scrapyards. Here, P-40s with their engines remove have been stacked upright in a field at the Reconstruction Finance Corporation's storage depot at Walnut Ridge, Arkansas, awaiting salvaging in October 1945.

Among the thousands of aircraft to meet the smelter at Walnut Ridge was this TP-40N, already shorn of its engine and suspended from a crane.

CHAPTER 13
XP-40Q

As World War II entered its final year, management at Curtiss realized that other USAAF fighters had overshadowed their P-40 fighter, especially in high-altitude combat performance. The XP-40Q was Curtiss' attempt to make the Warhawk competitive with the likes of the P-38, P-47, and P-51. Curtiss produced three experimental aircraft designated the XP-40Q, and all of them were powered by the Allison V-1710-121 engine with a two-stage, two-speed supercharger that provided significantly better performance at high altitude. Shown here is the second XP-40Q, designated XP-40 Q-2-CU. It was based on the airframe of the first P-40K-1-CU, 42-45722. *National Museum of the United States Air Force*

Faced with increasingly able competition, both against enemy aircraft as well as from other manufacturers vying for Army Air Force contracts, Curtiss undertook an extensive revision of the P-40, resulting in the XP-40Q.

Three prototypes of this aircraft were produced, all by converting earlier aircraft. The first XP-40Q was built from P-40K-10-CU 42-9987. It, like the other two XP-40Qs, would be powered by the Allison V-1710-121 engine, which had a War Emergency power rating of 1,800 horsepower. The aircraft featured a thickened wing center section housing the engine radiator. During testing the aircraft was further extensively modified with the rear fuselage cut down and a bubble canopy installed. This aircraft ground-looped at Wright Field in July 1944, and was subsequently written off.

The second prototype, 42-45722, was converted from the first P-40K-1-CU. This was an extensive rebuild, not only involving a change in engine and cowl, but also lengthening the fuselage by twenty inches and fitting a bubble canopy.

The third and final XP-40Q prototype was converted from P-40N-25-CU 43-24571, which had previously been modified with a cut-down spine and bubble canopy. It crashed during a test flight and was surveyed for salvage on September 11, 1944.

Despite promising performance, including a top speed of 422 miles per hour, no production of the P-40Q was carried out, the Mustang having secured its place as the USAAF's single-engine fighter of choice. The second XP-40Q was sold as surplus after the war and was entered into the 1947 Thompson Trophy race, during which it suffered a catastrophic engine failure, resulting in the crash of the plane.

The radiators of the XP-40Q-2-CU were moved from the chin of the fuselage to the wings, with air intakes on the leading edges of the wings outboard of the main landing gear. The oil cooler remained in the chin, with its air intake directly below the propeller. This plane also had a bubble-type canopy and windscreen, a long fuselage, and two .50-caliber machine guns in each wing. *National Museum of the United States Air Force*

The third XP-40Q, the XP-40Q-3-CU, as seen from the rear, was converted from P-40N-25-CU 43-24571. Like the XP-40Q-2-CU, it had a bubble canopy and lowered rear fuselage deck. This plane crashed during a test flight on September 11, 1944, two miles northeast of Eglin Field, Florida, but the pilot survived. However, the plane was beyond repair and was written off. *National Museum of the United States Air Force*

The second XP-40, XP-40Q-2-CU 42-45722, is viewed from the left side. The pitot tube was mounted on an L-shaped mast under the left wing. On the fuselage to the front of the leading edge of the wing is a rectangular duct with a door: probably a vent for air from the oil cooler.

One of the XP-40Qs, possibly the first one, 42-9987, flies ahead of a Curtiss C-46 transport plane. The XP-40Q was painted in a camouflage scheme of Olive Drab over Neutral Gray and had a shark's mouth and eyes on the nose. Despite proving its excellent performance, the Army declined ordering this model. *National Museum of the United States Air Force*